Pick a Pet

Write the right name to finish each sentence.

_____ has a cat.

_____ has a dog.

_____ has an odd pet. It is a zog!

Read the page again to check your work.

The Odd Pet

Read the sentences. Circle the right words to finish the sentences.

The zog is _____ .   It has ten red _____ .

fat / fan   logs / legs

It can _____ and hop.

rug / run

sit
It can _____ and beg.
set

          can   zog
Now Kim has a _____ and a _____ .
          cat   fog

Read the sentences again. Then colour the zogs.

Miss Hill's Maze

Well Done!
add sticker here
Well Done!

Get Miss Hill to the bus stop.
She can only go through words that rhyme with **hill**.

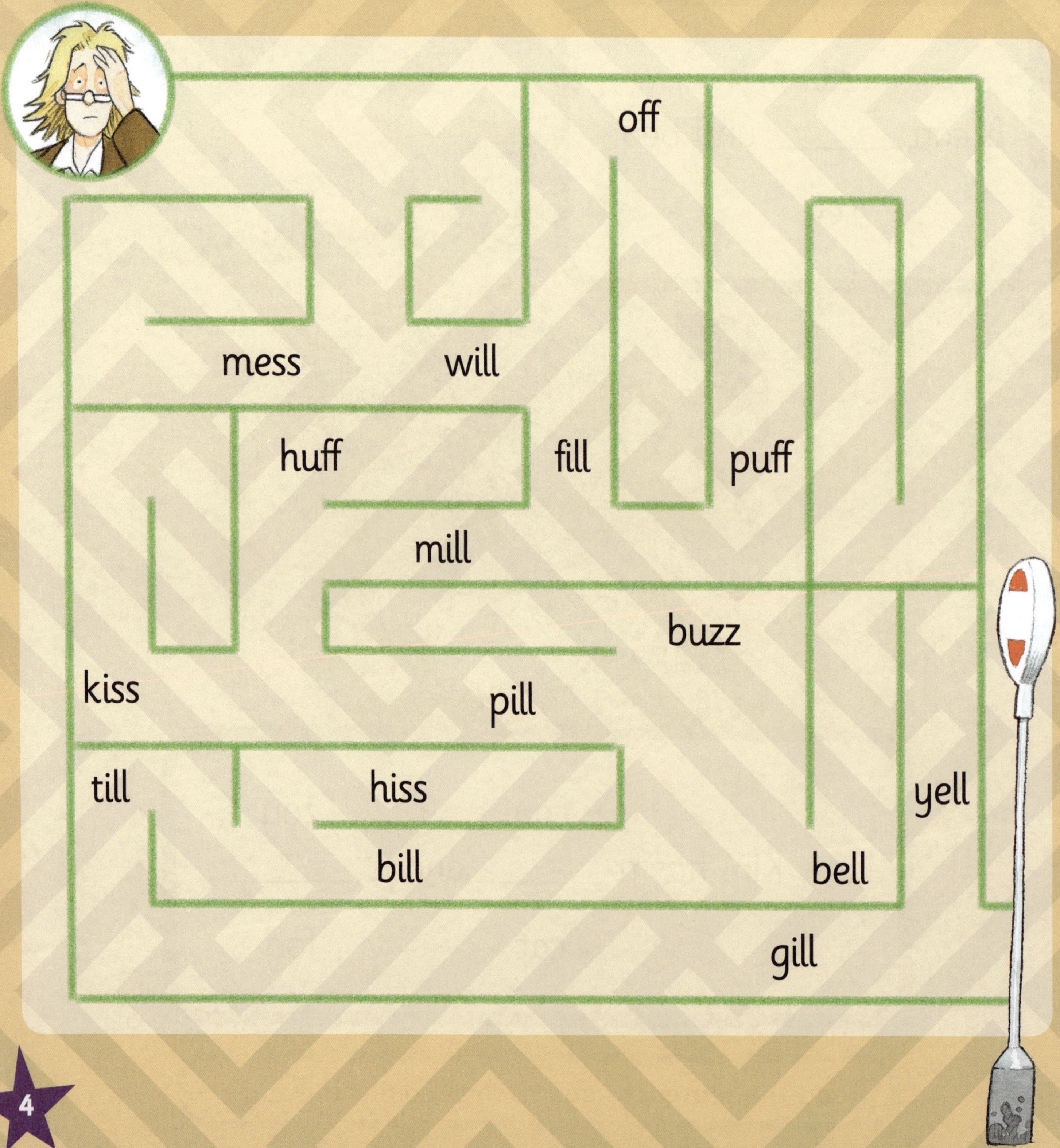
off
mess
will
huff
fill
puff
mill
buzz
kiss
pill
till
hiss
yell
bill
bell
gill

Missing Letters

Well Done!
add sticker here
Well Done!

The words on each shopping bag rhyme.
Write the missing letter to finish each word.
Use

e or i

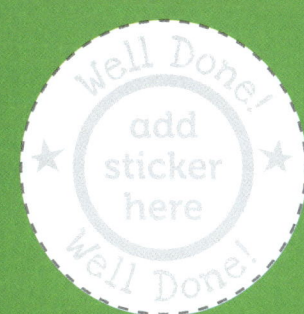

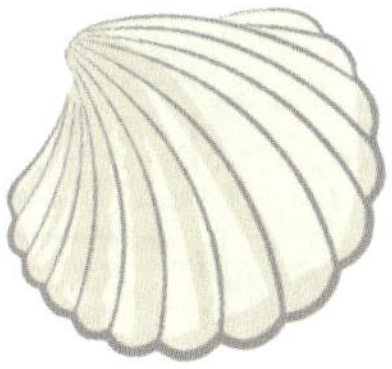

sh ___ ll

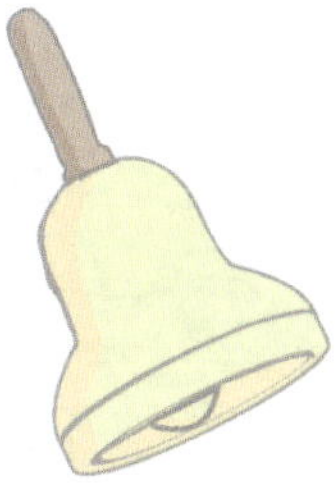

b ___ ll

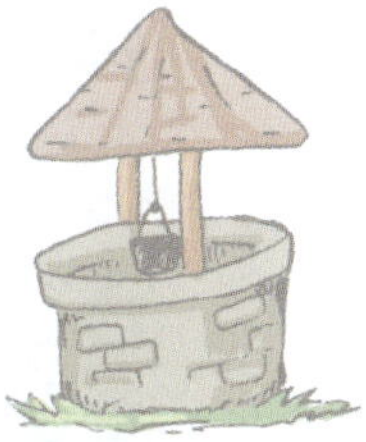

w ___ ll

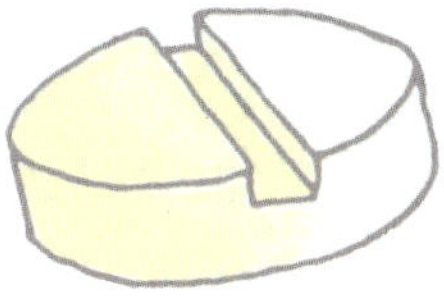

p ___ ll

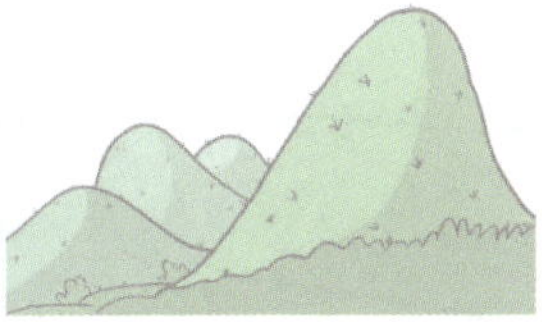

h ___ ll

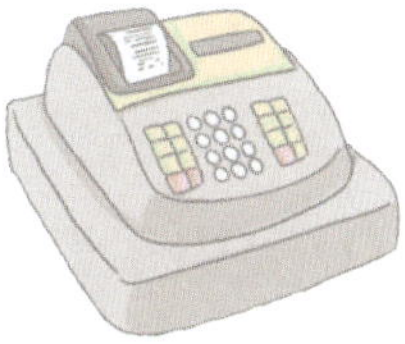

t ___ ll

Find the stickers to match the words.

This and That

Colour the picture. Then circle the right word to finish each sentence.

This is Mr Chan's ____ .
- shop
- ship

Mr Chan sells pens, pads and ____ .
- maps
- naps

This is Miss Thin's shop.

                            nuts

Miss Thin sells eggs, _____ and carrots.

                            nods

What things would you buy? Draw them in the basket.

Fish and Chips

Circle the right word to finish what is being said.

Sh or Ch?

Look at the pictures. Write the missing letters to finish each word.
Use sh or ch

fi ___

___ ip

___ op

___ in

di ___

___ ess

Find the stickers to match the words.

Doctor Duck

Read the sentences and underline the name of the person speaking. Then match the sentences to the right characters.

"Get up, Bob," said Dad.

"I am hot!" Bob said.

"Bob is sick!" said Mum.

"Quack, quack!" said Doctor Duck.

Mum

Dad

Doctor Duck

Bob

Can you act out the story?

Singing Dad

Read the sentences. Circle the right word to finish each sentence.

Dad sings to the cat and he sings to the _____ .

dug
dog

He sings in the sun and he sings in the _____ .

fog
fig

He sings in the shops and he sings in the _____ .

    shed
    shod

He sings in the bus and he sings in his _____ .

    bad
    bed

Read the sentences again. Which words rhyme?

Mr Zed

Read the sentences. Circle the right word to finish each sentence.

Patrick is _____ .
  six
  sit

He is having _____ with Jeff, Ellen and Wong-Jin.
  fan
  fun

Mr Zed has a top _____ .
  hit
  hat

"A rabbit is in it!" says Patrick.

Patrick _____ the hat and says, "Tick tack tock."

taps
tags

Will it be a rabbit?

No, it's _____ rabbits!

tin
ten

Read the sentences again. Then colour the picture.

Word Search

Read the words in grey and find them in the word search. Write over each word when you have found it.

| miss | off | doll | fell | things |
| huff | less | will | fuss | picks |

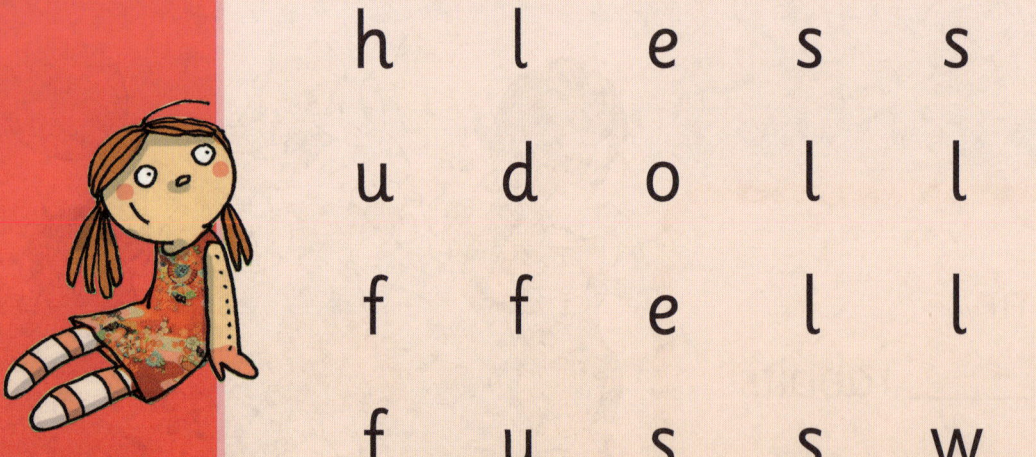

```
t  w  m  o  f  f  p
h  l  e  s  s  d  t
u  d  o  l  l  m  p
f  f  e  l  l  i  i
f  u  s  s  w  s  c
e  w  i  l  l  s  k
p  t  h  i  n  g  s
```

16

Stickers for page 5

Stickers for page 17

Stickers for page 10

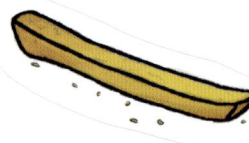 

Stickers for page 19

True or False?

Read each sentence. Then circle the right answer.

A bat has six wings.	**yes**	**no**
Camels have long legs.	**yes**	**no**
A rabbit can hop.	**yes**	**no**
Robins can sing.	**yes**	**no**
A fox has ten legs.	**yes**	**no**
A wombat has a red back.	**yes**	**no**
Ducklings hatch from eggs.	**yes**	**no**

Draw your favourite animal.

Ron Rabbit's Egg

Well Done! add sticker here Well Done!

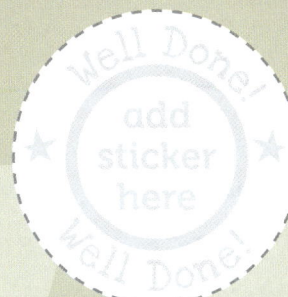

What is Ron Rabbit thinking?
Find a sticker to match each word.

hen

pot

hammock

racket

fish

jacket

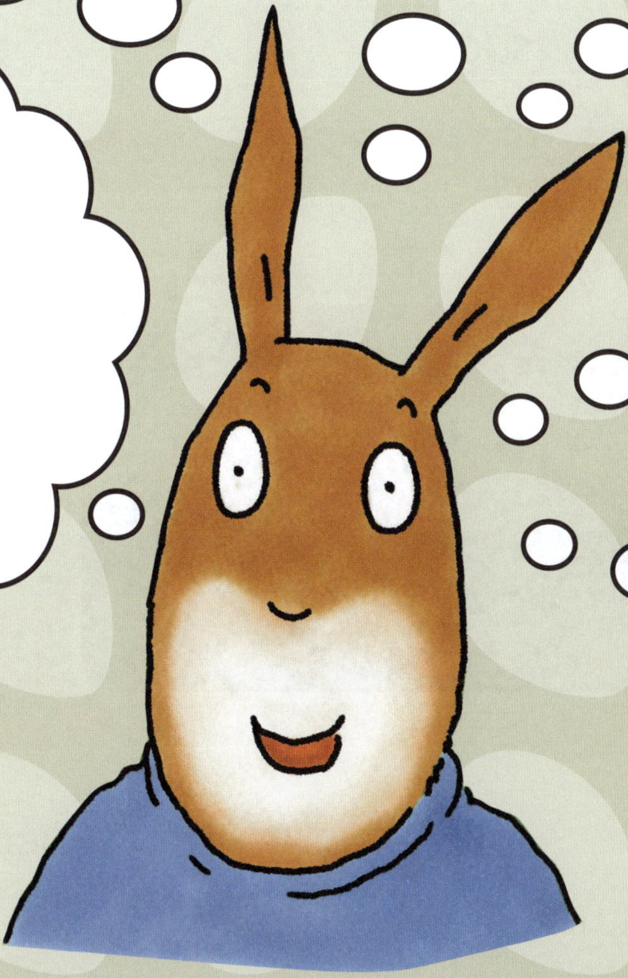

Read the words. Underline the words with a **ck** pattern.

The Ox and the Yak

Read the sentences. Circle the right words to finish the sentences.

On the back of an ox _____ a man with a _____ .
- sat / sack
- boss / box

On the _____ of a yak sat a man with a _____ .
- back / bang
- peck / pack

deck   hat
The men had a chat and the _____ got a _____ .
duck   hot

on   sing
Then the man with the _____ sang a very long _____ .
ox   song

Read the sentences again. Then check your work.

The Seven Kids

Write the right word to finish each sentence.
Use each of these words only once.

cut   sack   rocks   box

The fox puts six kids in his _____.

Ken kid

But Ken kid is in a _____.

Mum and Ken _____ the sack.

Mum and Ken put six _____ in the sack.

The Shopping List

Read the words. Look for the objects in the picture and write over the words when you have found them.

belt   lamp   bag   box   doll

dog bed   fish tank   milk   hat

Read the page again to check your work.

The Scrap Rocket

Label the picture.
Use **tin**, **lid**, **pot**, **tap**, **string**, **pump**, **plank**

Ask an adult if you can use some old pots and boxes to make your own rocket!

25

Gran is Cross

Write the right words to finish the sentences.
Use frog   snack   pram   twins

Flick brings a _____ .
Fred brings a _____ .

Gran gets the _____
a _____ .

Use cross   grabs   jumps   clock

The frog _____ in the jam.
Fred _____ him.

The frog jumps on the _____ .
Gran is _____ .

Read the sentences. Then check your work.

The 'ee' Tree

Write the missing letters to finish the words on the tree.
Use ee

thr____

gr____n

b____

sw____t

sh____p

wh____l

Read the words and match them to the right pictures.

Bob Bug and the Insect Club

Write the right word to finish each sentence.
Use brings   chicken   toast

Ant brings some _____.

Moth _____ some nuts.

Mum gives Bob some roast _____.

Which snack would you like? _____

Where is the Snail?

Read each sentence.
Then circle the right answer.

A chimp swings.   **yes   no**
A pink flamingo flaps its wings.   **yes   no**

A boat sails.   **yes   no**
A crab runs across a rock.   **yes   no**

A dog sits on his tail. yes no
A rabbit munches a parrot. yes no

Seven fish swim along. yes no
An octopus lies in wait. yes no

Find ten snails in the pictures.

Rails in the Rain

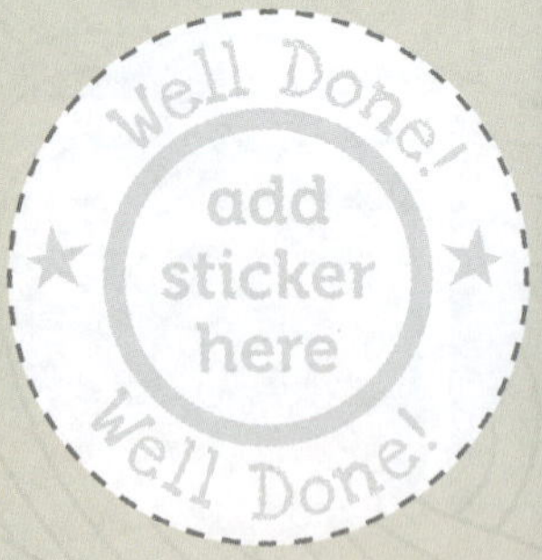

Write the missing letters to finish the words on the rail.

Use **ai**

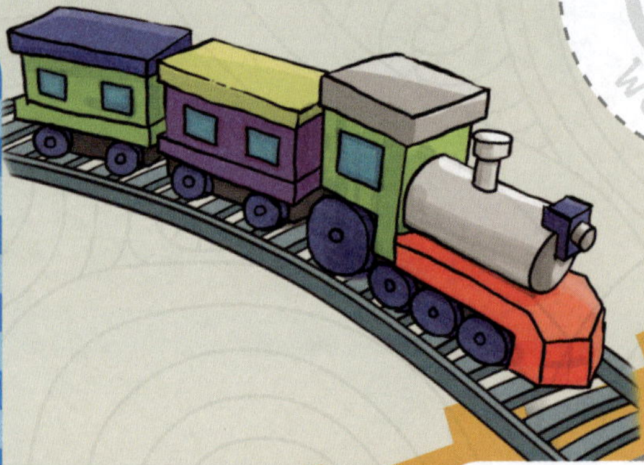

r_____n

tr_____n

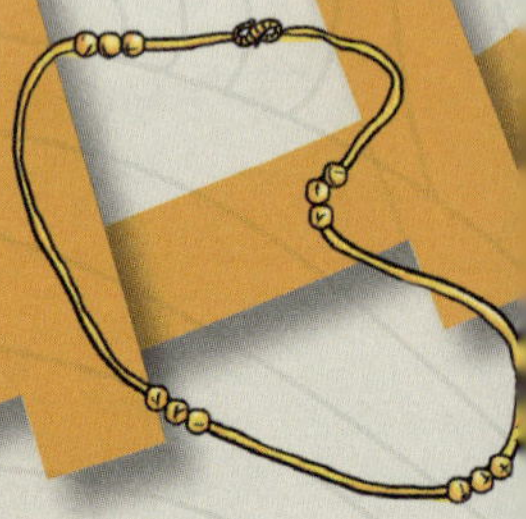

ch_____n

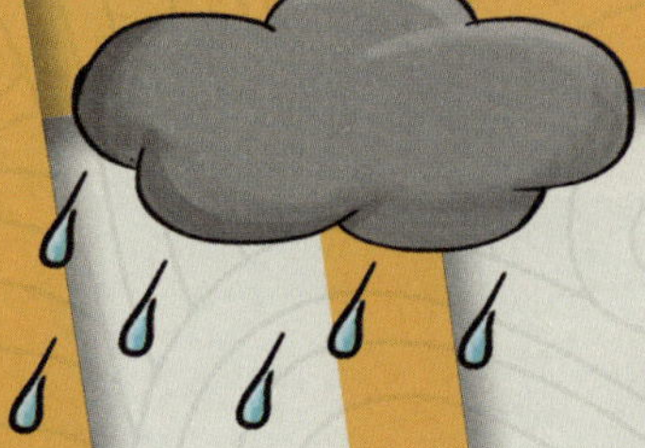

p_____nt

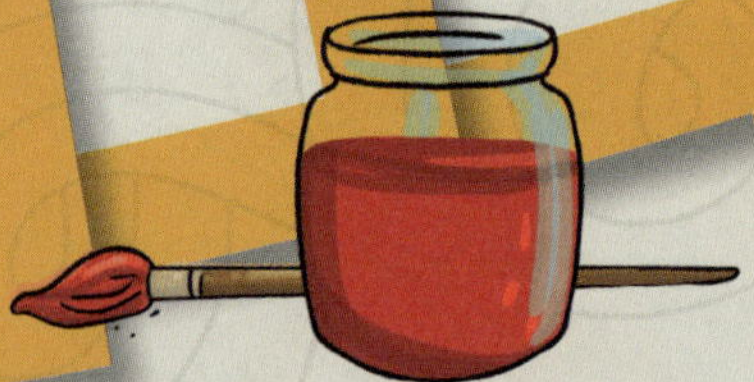

Read the words and match them to the right pictures.